The Rocky Mountains

By Molly Aloian

🌳 Crabtree Publishing Company

www.crabtreebooks.com

Crabtree Publishing Company

www.crabtreebooks.com

Author: Molly Aloian
Editor: Adrianna Morganelli
Proofreader: Kathy Middleton
Indexer: Wendy Scavuzzo
Designer: Katherine Berti
Photo researcher: Katherine Berti
Project coordinator: Kathy Middleton
**Production coordinator &
prepress technician**: Katherine Berti

Front cover: Moraine Lake is a glacier-fed lake
located in the Canadian Rocky Mountains in
Banff National Park, Alberta.

Title page: The Rocky Mountains in British
Columbia, Canada, are so high that snow
remains on the peaks even during the
summer months.

Picture credits:
Adobe Image Library: p. 44 (sheep)
Dreamstime: p. 26
Gemvision.com: p. 40 (sapphire)
Samara Parent: p. 5
Photos.com: p. 6 (fox)
Shutterstock: cover, p. 1, 4, 6 (mountain), 8–9 (mountain
    goat), 10, 11, 12, 13 (top_, 14, 15, 16, 17, 18, 19, 21, 22, 23,
    24, 25, 27, 28, 29, 30, 31, 32, 33, 35 (column), 38, 39, 40
    (mine), 40 (oil rig), 41, 42, 44 (wolf) , 45
Wikimedia Commons: 17 Avenue: p. 36 (statue); Lindsey
    Bengtson: p. 20; Albert Bierstadt: p. 37 (mountains);
    Charvex: p. 35 (sculpture); Anthony Finley: p. 8 (map);
    Friend of Smith—First published in Maurice Sullivan,
    The Travels of Jedediah Smith: p. 37 (portrait); David Herrera:
    p. 7; Kmusser: p. 36 (map); Ian Mackenzie: p. 34 (river);
    National Portrait Gallery (Great Britain): p. 34 (portrait);
    United States Geological Survey: p. 13 (bottom); Benjamin
    Zingg: p. 35 (column detail)

Library and Archives Canada Cataloguing in Publication

Aloian, Molly
    The Rocky Mountains / Molly Aloian.

(Mountains around the world)
Includes index.
Issued also in electronic formats.
ISBN 978-0-7787-7563-8 (bound).--ISBN 978-0-7787-7570-6 (pbk.)

    1. Rocky Mountains--Juvenile literature. I. Title. II. Series:
Mountains around the world (St. Catharines, Ont.)

F721.A46 2011   j917.8   C2011-905237-7

Library of Congress Cataloging-in-Publication Data

Aloian, Molly.
    The Rocky Mountains / Molly Aloian.
        p. cm. -- (Mountains around the world)
    Includes index.
    ISBN 978-0-7787-7563-8 (reinforced library binding : alk. paper) -- ISBN 978-
0-7787-7570-6 (pbk. : alk. paper) -- ISBN 978-1-4271-8844-1 (electronic PDF) --
ISBN 978-1-4271-9747-4 (electronic HTML)
    1. Natural history--Rocky Mountains--Juvenile literature. 2. Rocky
Mountains--History--Juvenile literature. 3. Rocky Mountains--Environmental
conditions--Juvenile literature. 4. Mountain life--Rocky Mountains--Juvenile
literature. I. Title. II. Series.

QH104.5.R6A46 2012
578.0978--dc23
                                              2011029832

Crabtree Publishing Company

www.crabtreebooks.com   1-800-387-7650

Printed in Canada/092011/MA20110714

Published in Canada
Crabtree Publishing
616 Welland Ave.
St. Catharines, Ontario
L2M 5V6

Published in the United States
Crabtree Publishing
PMB 59051
350 Fifth Avenue, 59th Floor
New York, New York 10118

Published in the United Kingdom
Crabtree Publishing
Maritime House
Basin Road North, Hove
BN41 1WR

Published in Australia
Crabtree Publishing
3 Charles Street
Coburg North
VIC 3058

CONTENTS

Words that are defined in the glossary are in **bold** type
the first time they appear in the text.

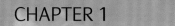

CHAPTER 1
The Backbone of North America

The magnificent Rocky Mountains are located in the western part of North America. They extend for more than 3,000 miles (4,828 km), stretching from northern Alberta and British Columbia in Canada down south to New Mexico in the United States. The Rockies are part of the American Cordillera, a collection of mountain ranges that run from Alaska all the way down to the tip of South America. For many years, artists have celebrated the natural beauty of the Rocky Mountains in art, films, and songs.

In the Beginning

The Rocky Mountains are millions of years old, but they are still among the youngest mountains in North America. They began to form more than 75 million years ago during the time of the dinosaurs. They began forming when part of Earth's **crust** under the Pacific Ocean slammed into the crust of North America. The edges of the crusts were very slowly pushed upward into tall mountains. Most of Earth's largest mountain ranges, including the Himalayas, the Andes, and the Alps, were formed in this way.

FAST FACT

The name Rocky Mountains comes from the Cree name *as-sin-wati*.

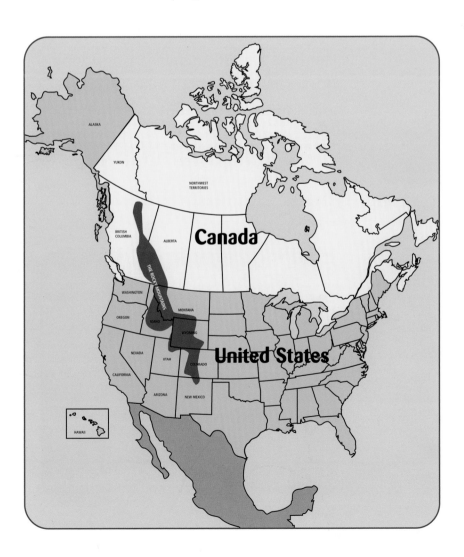

What is a Mountain?

A mountain is a gigantic natural landform that rises above Earth's surface. A mountain often has steep sides rising to a summit, which is the highest point or peak. Mountains are usually found in long ranges or groups of ranges called chains. They are formed in different ways, but most of the mountains on Earth have formed over millions of years. You may not be able to notice or feel it, but mountains are forming even as you read this book!

Impact on Earth

Over time, the Rocky Mountains have impacted Earth in a number of ways. They affect the **climate** over a huge area, including wind, rain, and temperature. They also control the flow of rivers and the water supply to many areas. In fact, the Rockies have their own climate. They are colder and windier than the low-lying lands beneath them. The air on the Rockies also contains less **oxygen** and lower humidity.

Tough Stuff

Rocky Mountain plants and animals are **adapted** to living in harsh mountain conditions. There are thousands of species of tough flowering plants on the Rocky Mountains. Different types of trees grow at different **elevations**. However, no trees can grow above the tree line, or **timberline**, because the conditions are simply too cold and windy. Mountain lions, red foxes, bighorn sheep, grizzly bears, and other animals are found throughout the Rocky Mountains. Their bodies have adapted to the climate. For example, the red fox has a large, fluffy tail that can be up to 20 inches (51 cm) long. It uses its tail for balance as it runs and jumps throughout the mountains.

When resting, the red fox uses its tail as a warm cover to protect it from cold weather.

Sacred Mountain

Ancient civilizations often believed that mountains were **sacred**. For example, ancient Japanese civilizations regarded Mount Fuji as sacred and ancient African civilizations regarded Mount Kenya as sacred. The ancient Greeks believed that their gods lived at the top of Mount Olympus in northern Greece.

Chief Mountain, visible in Montana and Alberta, is a landform of the Rocky Mountains that is held sacred by the Blackfoot people.

The Tallest Peaks

The highest peaks of the Rocky Mountains are found in the southern part of the mountain range. In Colorado, at the southern end of the Rockies, many peaks are more than 10,000 feet (3,048 m) tall. In the northern part of British Columbia, where the Rockies begin, most peaks are less than 9,500 feet (2,896 m) high.

FAST FACT

Within the Rockies, there is a variety of other landforms and **eco-regions** including foothills, plains, plateaus, deserts, and canyons.

Mount Elbert in Colorado is the highest peak in the Rockies. It measures 14,440 feet (4,401 m) high.

Mountain Exploration

The Rocky Mountains were one of the last regions of North America to be explored by Europeans. This was because the terrain was so rugged and difficult to access. Roman Catholic missionaries and various explorers began trekking through the mountains in the 17th and 18th centuries.

Surveyors and fur traders also explored the mountains to find routes and to set up trading posts. Today's geologists are still exploring the Rocky Mountains because of their abundant deposits of **fossil fuels** and other **minerals**. Geologists are scientists who study the structure of Earth and how it was formed.

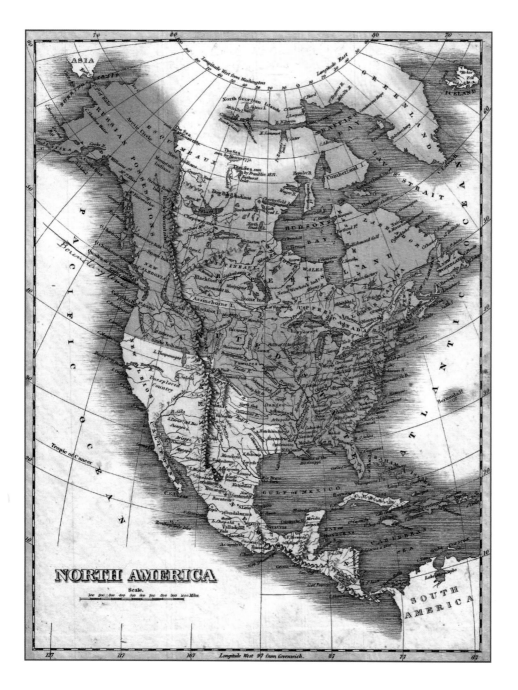

NORTH AMERICA

Scale.

This map from an atlas published in 1827 details the Rocky Mountains after exploration by the Spanish and Catholic missionaries.

While visiting the Rocky Mountains, tourists are able to get close to the wildlife, such as this mountain goat.

Human Presence

Both the seasonally harsh climate and rugged landscape have made human settlement limited in the Rocky Mountains. People still visit and live in the mountains, however. Today, there are **regulations** that ban hunting in the national parks and other areas within the mountains. These laws help to protect the unique mountain plants and animals. It also means that millions of tourists and other visitors can view the many mountain plants and animals in their natural habitats.

FAST FACT

Throughout the 1800s, fur trappers called "mountain men" furthered exploration of the Rockies through their hunting. The trails they built to transport the furs would later be used by settlers migrating west through the mountains.

Many Mountains

There are mountains all over the world on every single continent and in nearly every single country. Approximately 20 percent of the total land area on Earth is made up of mountains. There are even underwater mountain ranges. The mid-Atlantic Ridge, the longest mountain range on Earth, extends through the Atlantic Ocean. The mid-Atlantic Ridge forms a giant letter C between South America and Africa.

CHAPTER 2
How Did the Rockies Form?

The Rocky Mountains stretch from northern New Mexico and into Colorado, Utah, Wyoming, Idaho, and Montana. In Canada, the mountain range extends along the border of Alberta and British Columbia. The Rockies began forming approximately 75 million years ago. They are still moving and changing, but they are changing much too slowly for you to notice!

Water and glaciers have eroded the Rocky Mountain range, forming peaks and deep valleys.

Moving Plates

The Earth's crust is divided into giant slabs of rock called **tectonic plates**. These plates do not stay in the same place. They are constantly moving, which causes earthquakes and volcanic eruptions on Earth. The plates may move very slowly, but the changes on Earth can be enormous. The plates sometimes push up against one another. This causes their edges to slowly force up into gigantic folds and wrinkles —what we know as mountains. The Rocky Mountains were formed in this way. However, in order to completely understand the process we must go back in time hundreds of millions of years.

FAST FACT

The term for the process of mountain building is orogenesis. It comes from the Greek words *oros*, meaning mountain, and *genesis*, meaning creation.

Earth's Layers

Earth is made up of different layers of rock. The outermost layer of Earth is called the crust. Below the crust is the mantle, which is a very thick, dense layer of rock. The mantle is approximately 1,800 miles (2,897 km) thick—much thicker than the crust. The outer core is the next layer. The temperature of the outer core is very hot, but the inner core is even hotter. The temperature of the inner core is about 9,000°F (4,982°C).

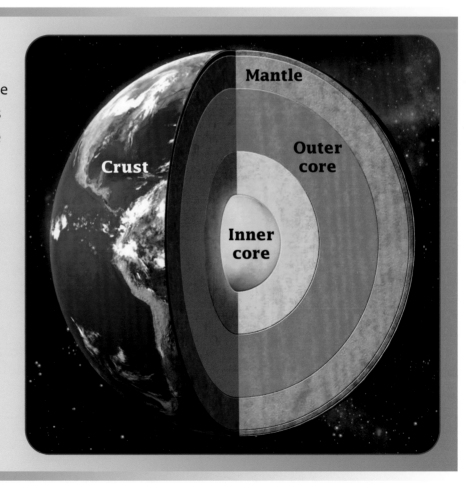

Mantle

Crust

Outer core

Inner core

Underwater

Around 700 million years ago, during the **Precambrian era**, the Pacific Ocean covered most of present-day North America. The Precambrian era is one of Earth's first eras of time. During this era, water covered most of today's western states and provinces. The ocean flooded, and then receded several times during the next 500 million years. Each time the ocean flooded, it left layers of **silt** and sand on the ocean floor. These layers built up higher with each flooding. Starting approximately 550 million years ago, water-dwelling **invertebrates** and the first **crustaceans** were living in the oceans. As these **organisms** died and sank to the ocean floor, they added to the layers of sediment. Over time, the increasingly heavy layers of sediment pressed down on the layers underneath and turned them into rocks such as sandstone, shale, and quartzite.

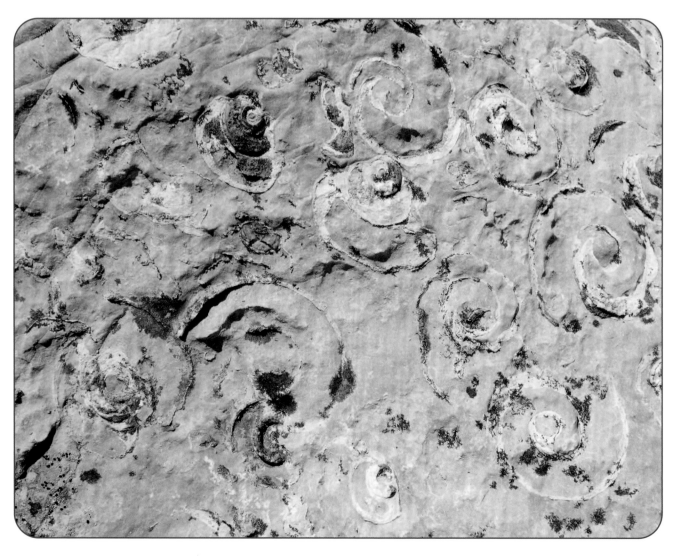

Dead animals and plants buried under sediment were turned into fossils after millions of years of pressure .

Taking Shape

Approximately 200 million years ago, the ocean floor along the west coast of present-day North America became unstable and began to waver. Around 75 million years ago, the crust under the Pacific Ocean bulldozed into the crust under western North America. The land at this **subduction zone** was crumpled and thrust upward, creating the Rocky Mountains. The layers of sediment that had accumulated on the ocean floor over hundreds of millions of years were folded, twisted, and squeezed. Gigantic slabs of rock broke away. In some places, older layers of rock were pushed on top of younger layers of rock. By the beginning of the **Tertiary period**, around 65 million years ago, the contours of today's Rocky Mountains were established and the mountains had taken shape.

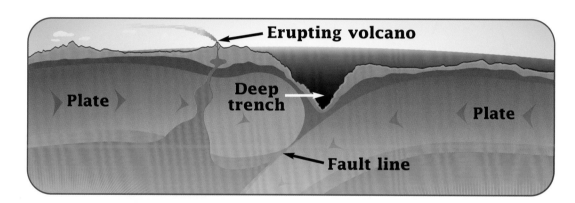

Erupting volcano

Plate

Deep trench

Plate

Fault line

When tectonic plates collide at a fault line, their edges push up into folds and wrinkles, creating mountains, valleys, and sometimes volcanoes.

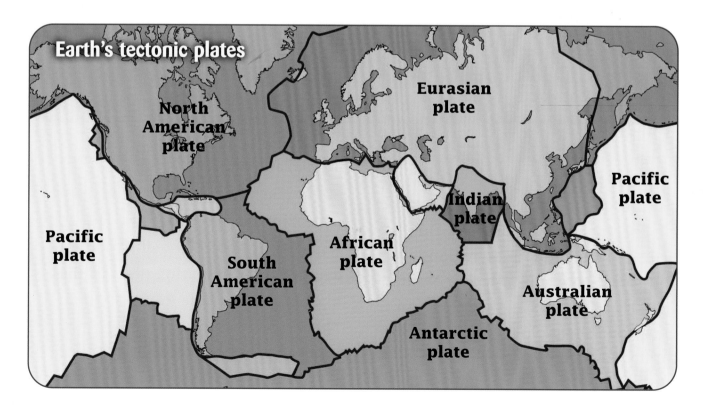

Earth's tectonic plates

North American plate

Eurasian plate

Pacific plate

Pacific plate

Indian plate

African plate

South American plate

Australian plate

Antarctic plate

The silt in Grinnell Lake, which is located in Glacier National Park, in Montana, gives it an opaque, turquoise appearance.

Ice Ages

Around one million years ago, Earth's climate cooled a few degrees. Huge glaciers formed in Arctic regions and slowly moved south over North America and Eurasia. A glacier is an enormous sheet of ice. These glaciers formed and then melted four more times. These time periods are known as glaciations or ice ages. The last major glaciation began moving south approximately 35,000 years ago. A glacier up to 6,560 feet (2,000 m) deep covered everything except the highest peaks of the Rocky Mountains. The ice scraped over the landscape, destroying all plant-life as it crept slowly forward.

Fields of Ice

In the mountains, these glaciers carved bowl-shaped hollows into the slopes of the higher peaks. These hollows are called cirques. The ice sheets rounded off lower peaks and carved pre-glacier, V-shaped valleys into post-glacier, U-shaped valleys. The last ice sheet began to retreat around 12,000 years ago. This also drastically changed the landscape. The rocks and other **debris** that the ice had picked up as it moved forward melted out during the retreat. High ridges known as **lateral moraines** and **terminal moraines** were formed. Many of these moraines blocked the natural flow of water. As a result, water pooled and lakes began to form. **Meltwater** drained into rivers and streams.

The Ptarmigan Cirque is located in Kananaskis Country, in Alberta, Canada.

The Great Divide

Today, the Rockies form the Continental Divide of North America. The Continental Divide is the imaginary line that divides the flow of water between the Pacific Ocean and Atlantic Ocean. Rain or snow that drains on the east side of the Continental Divide flows toward the Atlantic Ocean. Any precipitation on the west side drains and flows toward the Pacific Ocean. Every continent except Antarctica has a continental divide.

Water Ways

Water has had a huge effect on the appearance of the Rocky Mountains. First, glaciers scoured and battered the mountains. Over several million years, the flowing water in rivers and streams carved out the landscape of the Rocky Mountains. The process continues today. For example, the mountain peaks forming the boundaries of Banff National Park include the entire upper watershed of the Bow River. A watershed is an area of land that carries water away from the land after snow and ice melt and rain falls. Its shape channels water into soil, groundwater, creeks, and streams, and the water slowly makes its way to larger rivers and eventually into oceans. The Bow River flows southward through Banff National Park and then heads east out of the mountains and into the Saskatchewan River system. These waters continue east to Hudson Bay and the Atlantic Ocean.

The water of Athabasca Falls, in Alberta, falls over hard quartzite and steps carved out of limestone.

FAST FACT

Today, the only remnants of the last ice age are the scattered ice fields along the Continental Divide, including the 125-square-mile (324 km²) Columbia Icefield. The Columbia Icefield's meltwater feeds streams and rivers that pour into the Arctic Ocean, Pacific Ocean, and Atlantic Ocean.

Rocky Mountain Trench

The Rocky Mountain Trench is a huge valley that extends for about 900 miles (1,448 km) from western Montana in the United States, south of Flathead Lake, through British Columbia, Canada, and into the headwaters of the Yukon River. The trench floor is between two and ten miles (3.2–16 km) wide and 2,000–3,000 feet (610–914 m) above sea level. The headwaters of several rivers, including the Kootenay River and Fraser River, are located in the Rocky Mountain Trench.

Visitors are able to enjoy scenic views at Kootenay National Park, in British Columbia.

NOTABLE QUOTE

"If mountains were animals, the Rocky Mountains would be a team of wild mustangs: bold, beautiful, and free."

—Sacred Rides Mountain Bike Adventures

CHAPTER 3

Rocky Mountain Weather

The weather in the Rocky Mountains varies greatly from north to south. In the northern part of the mountain range, the climate is chilly for most of the year. The very southern part of the Rockies is on the fringe of a **subtropical** zone, but the climate is still very cold at high elevations.

Storms in the Rockies come from the Pacific Ocean in the west. Blowing clouds from the west are forced upward by the steep rocky walls. As the clouds rise, the air inside them becomes colder and water falls as rain or snow. The clouds contain significantly less water as they pass over the top of the mountains on the eastern side.

Northern Rocky Mountain Weather

Winters are severe in the northernmost part of the Rockies. The average temperature during the coldest months—generally from November to March—is below 32°F (0°C) and the average temperature of the warmest months—June to August—still remains below 72°F (22°C). Summer days are often warm, while the nights are cool. Precipitation averages 20 to 40 inches (51–102 cm) per year and is concentrated in fall, winter, and spring. Summers are usually dry, because winds from the west draw the dry climate of the Pacific coast across the area. Snowfall in winter is heavy, and permanent snowfields and glaciers cover small areas.

Worn Down

As soon as any mountain forms, rainwater and freezing temperatures slowly wear the mountain down. This is called erosion. Rivers carve deep valleys into rocks. Wind blows soil and small bits of rocks away. When water freezes inside a crack in a mountain rock, it swells and can split the rock apart and break it into smaller pieces.

Avalanches can happen suddenly in the northern Rockies. Residents and tourists should be prepared so they know what to do in case one occurs.

Middle Rocky Mountain Weather

The climate in the middle parts of the Rockies is relatively mild, which is mainly because they are close to the Pacific Ocean. Temperatures in Canyon City, Oregon, range from just above freezing to 68°F (20°C). In the mountain valleys of Montana, January temperatures average about 10° higher and summer temperatures are between 5–10° lower than on the **Great Plains** just to the east. The average length of the growing season is about the same as on the Great Plains.

It is approximately 120 days. Temperature and snowfall in the middle regions of the Rockies vary greatly depending on the altitude. Winds blow in from the west, with much of their moisture coming from the Pacific Ocean. As a result, most of the middle portion of the Rocky Mountains is **semiarid**, which means it receives relatively little annual rainfall. Valleys get less than 20 inches (51 cm) of precipitation each year. They receive up to 30 inches (76 cm) in the mountains, mostly as snow.

Meltdown

Today's climate experts believe that Rocky Mountain glaciers will have melted by 2100. Researchers from the University of Northern British Columbia discovered that one-quarter of Alberta's glaciers melted between 1985 and 2005. The prediction is based on a natural glacial melting period that began in the 1800s, as well as **climate change** caused by humans.

Since 1850, the number of glaciers in Glacier National Park in Montana has melted from 150 to 25.

On a sunny day, Going-to-the-Sun Road can be a scenic drive across Glacier National Park. In winter, however, the road can be covered in up to 80 feet (24 m) of snow.

Hells Canyon is located along the border of eastern Oregon and western Idaho. At approximately 8,000 feet (2,438 meters) deep, it is North America's deepest river **gorge**. Parts are desert-like and parts are alpine, which makes the weather hard to predict.

NOTABLE QUOTE

"It's well underway and it's just a matter, as the decades go on, of the ice rolling uphill until it's out of sight."

—Shawn Marshall, climate change specialist and geophysicist

Southern Rocky Mountain Weather

The climate in the southernmost parts of the Rocky Mountains is **temperate** and semiarid. Average annual temperatures range from 35°F to 45°F (2°C to 7°C) in most of the region, and can reach up to 50°F (10°C) in the valleys. The climate in this southern region is influenced by the prevailing west winds and the general north-south direction of the mountains. The western slopes of the mountains receive more precipitation than the much drier eastern slopes.

Winter precipitation varies depending on the altitude. The total amount of precipitation is moderate, but precipitation is greater than on the plains to the east and west. In the highest mountains, a considerable part of annual precipitation is snow, although permanent snowfields and glaciers cover only relatively small areas. At the base of these mountains, there is only 10 to 20 inches (25 to 51 cm) of rainfall per year. At higher elevations, annual precipitation increases to 40 inches (102 cm), and average temperatures are lower.

The Arapaho people lived and hunted in the warm summer months in what is now Indian Peaks Wilderness in Colorado.

Rocky Mountain Climate Organization

The Rocky Mountains and surrounding areas have already experienced the effects of climate change, or disruption: less snow, less available water, and more droughts and wildfires. The Colorado-based Rocky Mountain Climate Organization works to reduce climate change and its effects. Part of the organization's **mission** is to reduce harmful **emissions** and provide long-term solutions to climate change in the American West. Municipal governments, Denver Water, and various non-profit organizations work together as partners.

An increase in wildfires in the Rockies means a decrease in dense forest and an increase in open woodland. This shift in the ecosystem impacts the wildlife that live there.

Watertanker planes are flown to the sites of wildfires to assist firefighters in containing and putting out the fires.

CHAPTER 4

Plants and Animals

Different types of plants and animals are found in different parts of the Rockies. For example, larches are a species of tree adapted to life in the coldest parts of the mountains, but gamble oaks are adapted to growing in areas with warmer temperatures. The plants and animals in the Rocky Mountains are different from north to south.

The larch's wood is tough, free of knots, and waterproof, making it a popular building material for yachts and boats.

No Trees

There are no trees on the very tops of the Rocky Mountains. Trees stop growing at a certain elevation called the tree line, or timberline. The timberline is lower in the north where the climate is cold, windy, and dry all the time. In northern British Columbia, the timberline is at about 5,000 feet (1,524 m). In Alberta, it is at about 6,500 feet (1,981 m). Farther south, the timberline is at about 9,500 feet (2,896 m) in Wyoming, and roughly 11,300 feet (3,444 m) in New Mexico.

The Alpine Tundra

There are different **vegetation zones** within the Rocky Mountains. The alpine tundra is a vegetation zone that starts at elevations between 11,000 to 11,500 feet (3,352 to 3,505 m). Alpine plants are adapted to the strong winds and cold temperatures. Many alpine plants are perennial, which means that they live for several years. Many of the flowering plants in the alpine tundra are covered in dense hairs to protect them from the freezing winds. Lichens cling to rocks on the tundra because the soil does not contain enough **nutrients** for these plants to grow.

The trees that grow near the timberline are often short, twisted, and bent from the force of the high winds. They are rarely taller than six feet (1.8 m), but they may be hundreds of years old. Bristlecone pines can live to be 1,700 years old.

Lichens are the most widespread plants living on the peaks of the Rockies.

25

Subalpine Forest

The subalpine forest starts at elevations between 9,000 and 11,000 feet (2,743 and 3,352 m). The subalpine forest is made up mostly of subalpine fir, Engelmann spruce, and limber pine. In high, windblown areas, limber pines often grow into unusual shapes. Engelmann spruce and subalpine fir, which grow straight and tall in the lower subalpine forests, become shorter and deformed closer to the tree line. The trunks may grow upward, but strong, cold, dry winds may destroy new growth on the windward side, leaving permanent growth only on the other side of the trunk. Trees with branches on only one side are often called banner trees or flag trees.

Fir and larch forests grow on the sides of the Kananaskis range of the Canadian Rockies in Alberta, Canada.

Montane Forest

Below the subalpine forest is the montane forest. This vegetation zone starts at elevations between about 5,600 and 9,500 feet (1,707 and 2,896 m). Aspen, Ponderosa pine, lodgepole pine, and Douglas fir grow at these elevations. Grasses and shrubs grow between the trees and, during warmer seasons, wildflowers including daisies, lupines, and columbines grow. Various willows, mountain alders, and water-birch grow along mountain streams or along the shores of lakes within the Rocky Mountains.

FAST FACT

The widest variety of plants and animals are found in the montane forest.

Trembling Aspen

Trembling aspens are tall, slender trees that grow to be approximately 82 feet (25 m) tall. Their smooth, round-to-triangular-shaped leaves quiver in just the slightest breeze. In autumn in the Rocky Mountains, the leaves of the trembling aspens turn yellowish-gold and bronze.

Aspens reproduce through their root system, which can survive thousands of years.

Animal Life

Deer, elk, mountain goats, red foxes, and bighorn sheep spend most of their time at the lowest elevations of the Rockies—in the valleys and wide canyon bottoms between mountains. In these areas, there is less snow and grasses and other foods are easier to find. Predators such as mountain lions, bobcats, wolves, wolverines, coyotes, and grizzly bears prey on deer, elk, and bighorn sheep. They also prey on the muskrats, beavers, otters, minks, gulls, and shorebirds that spend time near marshes, **sloughs**, and small lakes within the mountains.

The hoary marmot lives in the alpine and subalpine forest and prefers to live on south-facing mountainsides that contain loose rocks and lush green tundra plants. Hoary marmots live in groups called colonies. Colonies live at the bases of boulder-strewn slopes with numerous crevices leading to underground burrows.

Canada Lynx

The Canada lynx lives in the northern Rockies and is well-adapted to its mountain habitat. Its fur-covered paws are wide and padded, which help it roam easily over deep snow and protect it from the cold. The fur between a lynx's toes acts like a snowshoe and prevents the lynx from sinking into the snow. Sharp, retractable claws help the lynx catch prey and climb up rocky mountain slopes. The Canada lynx can grow to be more than three feet (0.9 m) long and weigh over 35 pounds (15.9 kg).

The bighorn sheep is named for its large horns, which can weigh up to 30 pounds (14 kg).

Great Grizzly

Grizzly bears wander through many areas of the Rockies, but they commonly live in the alpine zone. There, they dig up the roots of plants, such as glacier lilies and peavines, for food. Thick shoulder muscles and long front claws help the bears dig through masses of earth for food. Grizzly bears also eat berries, plant shoots, small mammals such as rodents, and fish. Adult grizzlies can grow to be about eight feet (2.4 meters) tall and can weigh up to 900 pounds (408 kg)! During late summer and autumn, grizzlies eat as much as they can to accumulate large amounts of fat. They then spend winters in their dens.

Pass the Salt

Many Rocky Mountain animals visit natural salt licks in order to get the salt they need in their diets. Mountain goats, bighorn sheep, moose, elk, and deer visit areas where there are salty puddles of water and earth. They drink the water and eat the dirt in order to get the salt they need in their diets.

Bird Life

More than 300 different species of birds live in the Rocky Mountains. Various species of birds make nests in Rocky Mountain trees and find food in the neighboring meadows. Mountain bluebirds, robins, gray jays, hummingbirds, and flycatchers live close to the tree line. Noisy blackbirds, marsh wrens, and bitterns live in the cattails along the edges of mountain waterways. The harlequin duck looks for food in fast-flowing mountain streams and rivers. It dives underwater to feed on insects among the rocks and gravel.

Mountain bluebird

Bittern

Harlequin ducks

Gray jay

The water in Rocky Mountain rivers often looks gray and muddy. This is because the water contains tiny bits of rock dust called rock flour.

CHAPTER 5

People in the Rocky Mountains

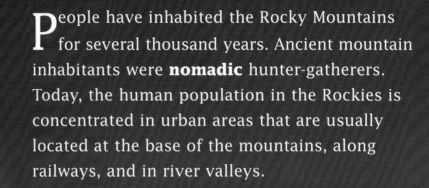

People have inhabited the Rocky Mountains for several thousand years. Ancient mountain inhabitants were **nomadic** hunter-gatherers. Today, the human population in the Rockies is concentrated in urban areas that are usually located at the base of the mountains, along railways, and in river valleys.

Snowboarders from all over the world visit resort towns near the Rockies.

Breckenridge, Colorado is a ski resort town with many part-time residents who own vacation homes there.

Paleo-Indians

The Rocky Mountains were once home to Paleo-Indians. Over 10,000 years ago, after the last ice age, these first peoples crossed the Bering Strait from Asia into North America. They were hunter-gatherers who were following large herds of plant-eating animals including caribou and the now-extinct mammoth. Paleo-Indians were nomadic, which means they moved from place to place as the seasons changed. They hunted animals in the foothills and valleys of the Rocky Mountains.

Indigenous Peoples

Indigenous peoples, including the Apache, Arapaho, Bannock, Blackfoot, Cheyenne, Crow, Flathead, Shoshone, Sioux, Ute, and others, lived in the Rocky Mountains after the Paleo-Indians. They entered the mountain ranges in the spring and summer to hunt deer and elk, to catch fish in the mountain waterways, and gather berries and other foods. Other indigenous peoples living in the mountains included the Shuswap and Kootenay of British Columbia, the Coeur d'Alene and Nez Perce of Idaho, and the Flathead of Montana. The traditional lands of the Shoshone in Idaho and Wyoming and the Ute in Utah and Colorado extended into the west-central mountain ranges. Today, many of these indigenous peoples still live in communities within the Rockies.

Many indigenous peoples carved totem poles from tall trees. These sculptures recounted events, clan histories, and legends.

NOTABLE QUOTE

"The mountains, I become part of it... The herbs, the fir tree, I become part of it. The morning mists, the clouds, the gathering waters, I become part of it."

—Navajo Chant

Spanish Exploration

A Spanish explorer named Francisco Vásquez de Coronado entered the Rocky Mountain region from the south in the 1540s. He traveled through parts of the Rockies with a group of soldiers, missionaries, and slaves from Africa. His expeditions resulted in the discovery of many landmarks such as the Grand Canyon. However, de Coronado and the members of his expedition forever changed the lives of the indigenous peoples that had been living there for thousands of years by introducing new cultures—and new diseases—into the area. De Coronado and other explorers forced the Native peoples to leave their traditional lands and hunting grounds.

Missionaries in the Mountains

In the 17th and 18th centuries, Roman Catholic missionaries began exploring the Rocky Mountains. They worked their way north from Mexico into New Mexico. In 1776–77, a Spanish missionary and explorer named Silvestre Vélez de Escalante documented an expedition into present-day Utah.

Sir Alexander Mackenzie

In 1792-93, the Scottish explorer and fur trader Alexander Mackenzie crossed the Rockies while searching for a waterway to the Pacific Ocean from the Canadian prairies. He found a route to the Arctic, but not the Pacific Ocean. The Mackenzie River, the longest river in Canada, is named in his honor.

During the winter, the Mackenzie River freezes over, and portions of it are used as ice roads.

Alexander Mackenzie

Lewis and Clark

In 1804–06, a United States military expedition called the Lewis and Clark Expedition explored and charted a route up the Missouri River into Montana and then across Idaho and Oregon to the Pacific Ocean. This expedition was led by Captain Meriwether Lewis and Lieutenant William Clark. It was a key part in the history of the exploration of America and westward expanison.

The Astoria Column at the mouth of the Columbia River in Oregon **commemorates** Lewis and Clark's expedition called the Corps of Discovery.

Sacagawea was a Shoshone woman who acted as an interpreter for Lewis and Clark on their expedition. Her role was important in easing tensions during first contact with different Native peoples.

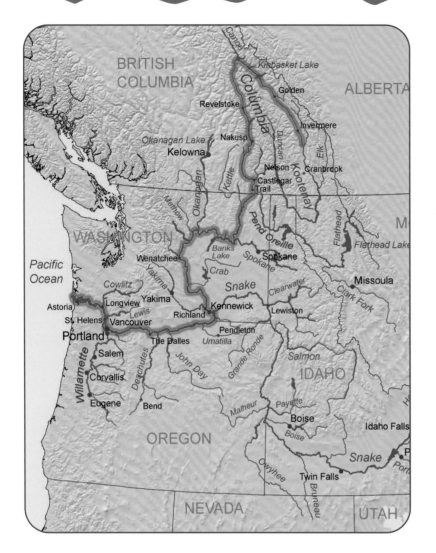

Mapping the Rockies

In 1807–11, the British explorer and fur trader David Thompson explored the headwaters of the Saskatchewan River and Columbia River in the Canadian Rockies. He set up the first trading posts in that region and produced the first survey of the entire length of the Columbia River. The maps he made of western North America were the basis of all subsequent maps of the area.

Thompson mapped about 1.5 million square miles (3.9 million km²) of wilderness over his lifetime—roughly one-fifth of North America.

Located on the bank of Lac la Biche, in Alberta, this statue shows English explorer David Thompson sailing in a canoe with two guides.

Rocky Mountain House

Rocky Mountain House National Historic Site, near Rocky Mountain House, Alberta, commemorates the many fur-trading posts built between 1799 and 1864 by the North West Company and the Hudson's Bay Company near the North Saskatchewan River and Clearwater River. The site includes a visitor center and hiking trails.

Mountain Museum

The Whyte Museum of the Canadian Rockies, located in Banff, Alberta, collects, preserves, and exhibits educational materials related to the cultural heritage of the Rocky Mountains and other mountains around the world. The museum was the inspiration of Banff artists Peter and Catharine Whyte. The Whytes dedicated their lives to painting mountain wilderness and culture, and to collecting local art and historical material. Exhibitions at the Whyte Museum feature historical and contemporary art inspired by mountain cultures around the world. Ongoing exhibits explore the development of Banff and the history of the Rocky Mountains.

Jedediah Smith

In 1822, a trader and explorer named Jedediah Smith joined a fur trading expedition to the Rocky Mountains and became the first U.S. citizen to travel overland to California. Following the Missouri River into Montana, Smith worked his way south into the Bighorn Basin. He then entered southeastern Idaho, northern and southwestern Utah, and southern Nevada, around the Sierra Nevada, and then headed back to the Great Salt Lake across the Great Basin.

Albert Bierstadt (1830-1902) was an American landscape painter who joined many expeditions in order to capture the true essence of the American West.

CHAPTER 6

Natural Resources and Tourism

The Rocky Mountains are rich in **natural resources** including lumber, coal, natural gas, as well as deposits of copper, iron ore, silver, gold, lead, and other minerals. These resources contribute to the economic development of towns and cities within the Rockies. Millions of tourists also visit the Rockies each year to hike, camp, ski, snowboard, and participate in other mountain sports.

Resort areas throughout the Rockies provide vacationers with access to national parks such as Banff National Park (above).

Sawmills can be found throughout the Rockies.

Forestry

Much of the land in the Rockies has been designated as national forests or provincial forests. However, forestry is a major industry in the Rockies. Timber from the Rockies supplies numerous sawmills and paper mills. The Douglas fir is a very important tree in the lumber industry and is native to the Rocky Mountains. Wood from these trees is used for plywood, flooring, and other construction lumber. They are also used as Christmas trees because they retain their needles better than true firs and spruce trees.

Rocky Mountain Forest Products

Rocky Mountain Forest Products is the largest single supplier of exterior lumber products in the United States. They provide service across the United States, including Colorado, Wyoming, Utah, New Mexico, and Arizona and buy directly from lumber mills in the Pacific Northwest, California, Idaho, and Canada. The company's goal is to serve independent general contractors, small-scale home builders, remodelers, and fence and landscape companies.

Minerals

Copper is one of the most valuable resources within the Rocky Mountains. This mineral has been extracted from large mines in British Columbia, Montana, Utah, and Arizona. There are also many underground mines of silver, gold, lead, and zinc, which are found in British Columbia, Colorado, Montana, Idaho, Utah, New Mexico, and Arizona.

Extracting Oil

There are also plentiful deposits of rock called shale in the Rocky Mountains. Oil shales are found mainly around the Uinta Mountains in Wyoming, Colorado, and Utah. There is also oil in rocks called sandstone in various places throughout the Rockies. These deposits are sometimes called tar sands. Overall, the amount of potential oil in the Rockies is vast.

Sapphires are beautiful gemstones that are mined in the Rockies of Montana.

Silver is mined in Colorado, Nevada, and Idaho— the state that has mined the most silver.

Some oil drilling rigs are powerful enough to drill through thousands of meters of Earth's crust.

FAST FACT

Gold was discovered in Idaho, Colorado, Montana, and the Yukon in the 19th century.

The southern Alberta foothills of the Rockies have been a cattle ranching center since the 1870s.

Pikes Peak or Bust!

The Pikes Peak Gold Rush followed the California Gold Rush by approximately one decade. It is known today as the Colorado Gold Rush. It produced a huge increase of **immigrants** into the Pikes Peak Country of the southern Rocky Mountains.

The slogan for the rush was "Pikes Peak or Bust!" This was a reference to the prominent mountain at the eastern edge of the Rocky Mountains. It was this mountain that guided many early **prospectors** westward over the Great Plains to the Rocky Mountain region.

National Parks

Many of North America's most beautiful national parks and wilderness areas lie within the Rocky Mountains. Yellowstone National Park lies mostly in Wyoming with parts in Montana and Idaho. It is one of the largest temperate-zone ecosystems on Earth. Large numbers of tourists are drawn to the area each year by the large populations of elk, bison, and moose, as well as more than ten thousand **hot springs**. Rocky Mountain National Park in Colorado has majestic mountain views, forests thick with trees, tundra, and many species of wildlife. More than one million people visit this park and nearby towns and cities every year. Banff National Park in Alberta is Canada's oldest national park and contains numerous ice fields and glaciers for tourists to explore.

Lightning Fire!

On June 24, 2010, a wildfire burned over 2.4 square miles (6.1 square km) of the Rocky Mountain National Park in Larimer County near Estes Park. The Estes Park Fire Department believed that lightning may have started the fire.

A herd of bison moves along the Firehole River in Yellowstone National Park.

Keep the Sheep!

At the beginning of the nineteenth century, there were between 1.5 million to two million bighorn sheep in North America. Today, there are less than 70,000. Hunting, habitat loss, loss of food from livestock grazing, and diseases from domestic livestock devastated bighorn sheep populations. The Rocky Mountain National Park collaborates with the state of Colorado to protect the population of bighorn sheep throughout the Rockies.

Gray wolf

FAST FACT

Some Rocky Mountain plants and animals, including the Canada lynx and the gray wolf, are protected under the Endangered Species Act.

NOTABLE QUOTE

"America's national parks are the touchstones of our shared history and culture. In some ways, they represent the soul of the nation. They represent our hopes, our dreams, our struggles. They are our absolute best places."

—Tom Kiernan, President of the National Parks Conservation Association

Protecting the Rocky Mountains

Many of the ecosystems within the Rocky Mountains are extremely fragile and need to be protected. Tourism, industry, commercial and residential development, and pollution threaten the delicate webs of life within the Rocky Mountains. The National Parks Conservation Association (www.npca.org) is one organization whose mission is to enhance and protect America's national parks, including those within the Rockies, for present and future generations. Members educate decision makers and the public about the importance of preserving national parks. They also help convince members of congress to uphold the laws that protect the parks. In Canada, the Canadian Parks and Wilderness Society (www.cpaws.org) works toward keeping at least half of Canada's public land and water wild.

Not Allowed

Potentially destructive recreational activities are not permitted within certain areas of the Rocky Mountains. Off-road recreational vehicle use, bicycles on trails, and hang gliding or paragliding from mountaintops is forbidden.

The Lions Gate Bridge in Vancouver, British Columbia, was built in 1938.

Guided tours of the Columbia Icefield in Jasper National Park, Canada, allow tourists to skate, ski, and snowmobile.

TIMELINE

About 75 million years ago	The Rocky Mountains begin to form.
Around 65 million years ago	The contours of the mountains begin to take shape.
Around 35,000 years ago	Last major ice age
6000 B.C. to 150 A.D.	Nomadic hunter-gatherers are living throughout the Rocky Mountains. These people are ancestors of indigenous peoples including the Apache, Shoshone, and Comanche.
1540s	The Spanish explorer Francisco Vásquez de Coronado enters the Rocky Mountain region from the south.
1600s and 1700s	Roman Catholic missionaries explore the Rocky Mountains.
1776–1777	Silvestre Vélez de Escalante documents an expedition into Utah
1792–1793	Alexander Mackenzie crosses the Rockies while searching for a waterway to the Pacific Ocean
1804–1806	Lewis and Clark's Corps of Discovery expedition charts parts of the Rocky Mountains
1807-1811	British explorer and fur trader David Thompson produces the first survey of the entire Columbia River—the basis for all subsequent maps.
1822	Jedediah Smith becomes first white explorer to travel overland through Utah to California.
1858–1861	Pikes Peak Gold Rush in Colorado
1871	Addie Alexander is the first woman to climb Longs Peak in Colorado.
1872	Yellowstone National Park in Wyoming and Montana becomes the first national park in the world.
1887	Rocky Mountains Park (renamed Banff National Park in 1930) is created as Canada's first national park.
1915	Rocky Mountain National Park in Colorado is formally dedicated.
1966	In the United States, the National Historic Preservation Act protecting historic and prehistoric resources on federal land first takes effect.
1984	Yellowstone National Park declared a World Heritage Site by UNESCO.
1978	Kootenay and Yoho national parks in British Columbia, and Banff and Jasper national parks in Alberta are together declared a World Heritage Site by UNESCO.
2010	A wildfire burns over 2.4 square miles (6.1 km²) of the Rocky Mountain National Park in Colorado.

GLOSSARY

adapted Changed so as to fit a new or specific use or situation

climate The long-term weather conditions in an area

climate change A long-term, lasting change in the weather conditions in an area

commemorates Marks with a ceremony or special remembrance

crust The outer part of Earth

crustaceans A large group of animals, including lobsters, shrimps, and crabs, that live in water and have an exoskeleton

debris Fragments and rock and other materials

eco-region A large area of land or water containing a geographically distinct group of species, natural communities, and environmental conditions

elevations Heights that are above sea level

emissions Materials that are discharged

fossil fuels Fuel, such as coal, oil, or natural gas, that are formed inside Earth from plant or animal remains

gorge A narrow passage, ravine, or steep-walled canyon

Great Plains The elevated plains region in the western central United States and western Canada, east of the Rockies

hot springs Springs containing water that flows out at temperatures higher than the average temperature of the place where the springs are located

immigrants People who come to a country to live there

indigenous Living things that are naturally found in a particular region or environment

invertebrates A large group of animals that do not have backbones

lateral moraines Parallel ridges of debris deposited along the sides of a glacier

meltwater Water released by melting snow or ice

minerals Naturally occurring substances that come from the ground

mission A task or job

natural resources Materials found in nature that are valuable or useful to humans

nomadic Describing people that have no permanent homes and move from place to place

nutrients Materials that living things need to survive

organisms Living things

oxygen A colorless, tasteless, odorless gas, which forms about 21 percent of the atmosphere and is necessary for life on Earth

Precambrian era The earliest era of geological history

prospectors People who explore areas in search of valuable minerals

regulations Rules or orders

sacred Describing something that is deserving of respect or honor

semiarid Having light or minimal rainfall

silt Very small particles of sediment

subduction zone The place where two tectonic plates come together, one riding over the other

subtropical Describing regions that border on the tropical zone

tectonic plates Gigantic pieces of Earth's crust

temperate Describing a climate that is usually mild without extremely cold or extremely hot temperatures

terminal moraines Debris that is deposited at the end of a glacier

Tertiary period The earliest period of the Cenozoic era of geological history that is marked by the formation of high mountains and the importance of mammals on land

timberline The area of land above which no trees grow due to the harsh climate

vegetation zones Areas of land in which types of plants best survive

INDEX

FIND OUT MORE

BOOKS

Bauer, Marion Dane and Wallace, John. *The Rocky Mountains (Wonders of America)*, Simon Spotlight, 2006.

Cannings, Richard. *The Rockies: A Natural History*. Greystone Books; First Trade Paper Edition, 2007.

Graf, Mike and Leggitt, Marjorie. *Rocky Mountain National Park: Peril on Longs Peak*. Fulcrum Publishing, 2010.

Grupper, Jonathan. *Destination: Rocky Mountains*. National Geographic Children's Books, 2001.

Hamilton, John C. *Rocky Mountain National Park*. ABDO & Daughters, 2008.

Kurtz, Kevin and Hunter, Erin E. *A Day on the Mountain*. SylvanDellPublishing, 2010.

Lynch, Wayne. *Rocky Mountains (Our Wide World)*. Cooper Square Publishing Llc, 2006.

WEBSITES

Rocky Mountain National Park
www.nps.gov/romo/index.htm

Forest Biomes of North America— Rocky Mountain Evergreen Forest
http://forestry.about.com/library/tree/bl_na_biomes_rockymt.htm

Yellowstone National Park
www.nps.gov/yell/index.htm

Banff National Park of Canada
www.pc.gc.ca/pn-np/ab/banff/index.aspx

Rocky Mountain Tour Guide
www.rocky-mountain-tour-guide.com/animals.html

Bighorn Mountain Sheep
www.bcadventure.com/adventure/wilderness/animals/bighorn.htm

Wildlife of the Rocky Mountains
http://raysweb.net/wildlife/index.html